BITTER FRIENDS

by

Gordon Rayfield

SAMUEL FRENCH, INC.
45 West 25th Street   NEW YORK 10010
7623 Sunset Boulevard   HOLLYWOOD 90046
LONDON   *TORONTO*

BITTER FRIENDS

by

Gordon Rayfield

Samuel French, Inc.

GORDON RAYFIELD is the author of five plays, including *Fever of Unknown Origin*, which was produced by Neile Weissman at St. Clement's Theatre in New York City in 1988. *Bitter Friends* had its world premiere in January 1989 at the Jewish Repertory Theatre in New York City, directed by Allen Coulter. It has since been performed in Los Angeles, Cleveland, San Diego, Toronto, Jerusalem and Tel Aviv. His other plays, *The King of New Jersey, Thunderbunk,* and *The Numbers,* have been given readings at the Ensemble Studio Theatre, St. Clement's Theatre, and the Jewish Repertory Theatre, where he is a playwright-in-residence. Mr. Rayfield has also written for *A B C Afterschool Specials, AIDS Quarterly* on PBS, and for public television station WGBH-TV in Boston. His articles have appeared in *The New York Times, The Washington Monthly,* and other publications. Mr. Rayfield was the founder and first president of the Association of Political Risk Analysts, and is a member of the Dramatists Guild and the Writers Guild of America-East. He holds a Ph.D. in Political Science from City University of New York, where he wrote his dissertation on the Arab-Israeli conflict.

This play is dedicated to my mother and my father, and to Jean, who went without shoes.

IMPORTANT BILLING AND CREDIT REQUIREMENTS

Bitter Friends premiered in January 1989 at the Jewish Repertory Theatre, directed by Allen Coulter, with set design by Michael C. Smith; costume design by Laura Drawbaugh, lighting design by Dan Kinsley and sound design by Gary and Timmy Harris.

The cast (in order of speaking) was:

DAVID KLEIN......................Ben Siegler
RACHEL KLEIN.................Farryl Lovett
RABBI ARTHUR SCHAEFER.....Sam Gray
AMBASSADOR EZRA BEN-AMI
......................................Yosi Sokolsky
HELEN KLEIN ....Viola Harris
CONGRESSMAN FRANK FITZGERALD
....Bill Nelson
WINGATE WHITNEY.............Dan Pinto
EMBASSY EMPLOYEE, HEADWAITER,
GUARD ....Andrew Thain

CHARACTERS

DAVID KLEIN, about thirty, wears glasses, a careless dresser, with a look of distraction, of a mind occupied elsewhere. Strong-willed, unyielding and self-righteous, but can be emotionally vulnerable at times.

RACHEL KLEIN, his wife, late twenties, very attractive but isn't concerned about it. Friendly and practical, optimistic but easily wounded, has an intense and passionate loyalty to her husband.

RABBI ARTHUR SCHAEFER, early sixties, a stylish and expensive dresser. Distinguished, sophisticated, intellectual, a bit pompous and generally pleased with himself, but has a self-deprecating wit.

EZRA BEN-AMI, the Israeli ambassador, forties, wears poorly-fitted, inexpensive suits. Blunt, powerful-looking, a soldier, dour by nature, but can be warm, if guarded. Always working to control more explosive feelings.

HELEN KLEIN, David's mother, late fifties, aging but attractive in a stiff, reserved way. Wears dark, conservative clothes and never a hair out of place. Distrustful, tightly wrapped, feels cheated by life and profoundly resents it.

FRANK FITZGERALD, a congressman, fifties, casual, with an appealing, shaggy style. Cheerful and outgoing, with an Irish politician's heartiness and finely-honed instinct for self-preservation.

WINGATE WHITNEY, deputy attorney general, late thirties, wears expensive but unstylish clothes. Arrogant but edgy, undamaged by life and afraid to be found out.

VOICE AT THE EMBASSY, EMBASSY EMPLOYEE, JUDGE'S VOICE, HEADWAITER, GUARD

SETTING

The set should suggest an institutional building, exterior on one side, interior on the other, with high walls, marble floors, pillars, sconces. The stage is empty except for some interchangeable furniture: four chairs, a large table and a smaller one. Downstage to one side, clearly outside the action of the play, is a podium with five or six microphones.

SCENES

ACT I

ACT II

The characters and situations in this play are wholly fictional and do not portray, and are not intended to portray, any actual party or parties.

ACT I

Scene 1

The sound of TRAFFIC. LIGHTS UP fast on the gate outside the Israeli Embassy. DAVID and RACHEL run over to the gate. DAVID presses a buzzer and speaks into an intercom.

VOICE. Who is it please?
DAVID. My name is David Klein. I have to see Ephraim!
VOICE. Excuse me?
DAVID. I have to see Ephraim!
VOICE. Please repeat your name.
DAVID. David Klein!
VOICE. What is your business, please?
DAVID. I said, to see Ephraim!
RACHEL. David, is that the same car?
VOICE. Do you know his last name?
DAVID. No, but he works on the second floor! Ephraim!

(The sound of a CAR STOPPING.)

RACHEL. They're stopping—
VOICE. Please, one moment.
RACHEL. What's taking so long?

(*THEY both punch at the buzzer*.)

    DAVID. Hello? Hello!
    VOICE. This is Mr. Cohen?
    DAVID. Klein!

(*Offstage, the sound of CAR DOORS opening and slamming*.)

    RACHEL. It's those men, David!
    DAVID. What?
    RACHEL. Getting out of the car, the same men—
    VOICE. There is not anyone here named Ephraim.
    DAVID. There is, of course there is! I was in his office!
    VOICE. You must be a mistake—
    RACHEL. David, they're coming!
    DAVID. Tell him the FBI is after me, he told me to come to the Embassy!
    VOICE. I am sorry—
    RACHEL. David, we have to get out of here!

(*RACHEL grabs his hand but He pulls it away*.)

    DAVID. Wait!
    RACHEL. David!

(*THEY freeze. BLACKOUT*.)

Scene 2

*The sound of VOICES. LIGHTS UP on the
podium as SCHAEFER enters. The sound of
camera MOTOR-DRIVES as FLASHBULBS
pop. SCHAEFER waits a moment, then speaks
to the audience.*

SCHAEFER. According to the rabbis, the most
important questions are never answered. For
instance, the question, what is a Jew? The simple
answer is, a Jew is someone with a Jewish
mother. And you would think, that should be
enough, either you have a Jewish mother or you
don't. And believe me, this is something you find
out very early in life. But for ages Jews have
argued about this question, what is a Jew, and
still today we don't agree. But the rabbis also
said, don't worry about the answers, the
questions are more important. For us today,
however, in this age of information that we live
in, we want answers, fast. This is why, I know,
you're all here today, to get the inside story from
someone who was there, who knows what went
on behind the scenes. Which is where I've been
my whole life. I've never been the kind of rabbi
who spends his time contemplating the great
mysteries of the universe. I prefer the simpler
problems. Peace in the Middle East. Human rights
in the Soviet Union. If you need to solve a little
day-to-day kind of problem like that, Arthur

Schaefer is the rabbi for you. But the rabbis also say, the questions are more important than the answers. Which is what we're here for, after all, to ask the question of David Klein. The question of an American Jew who spied on the United States for Israel ...

(*SCHAEFER crosses upstage. LIGHTS DOWN on the podium.*)

Scene 3

LIGHTS UP on the lobby of a New York hotel. Offstage, the sounds of a CROWD in a ballroom. EZRA enters and hurries over to SCHAEFER.

EZRA. Arthur. So sorry I'm late ...
SCHAEFER. I was starting to worry you wouldn't get here at all.
EZRA. The shuttle was held in Washington. All the time on the runway I am having a vision, five hundred American Jewish leaders eat their dinner and go home.
SCHAEFER. They'd wait all night for the Israeli Ambassador, you know that. And just to make sure, we didn't give them dinner ...
EZRA. This is the reason they stay?
SCHAEFER. I'm joking, Ezra. I never saw people so upset about something that isn't a war

or a terrorist attack. They can't believe it, an American Jew stealing U.S. military secrets for you—

EZRA. Arthur, the boy of his own idea went to an Israeli in Washington, offering these plans, and this Israeli without telling anyone in authority accepted the plans.

SCHAEFER. But there are a lot of people saying you recruited him—

EZRA. It makes no difference what they say.

SCHAEFER. If he did it on his own, he's just an idealistic kid who went too far. If you recruited him, it's Israel spying on America—

EZRA. The State of Israel does not use Jewish citizens of any country for intelligence work.

SCHAEFER. Maybe hearing it from you, they'll start to believe it.

EZRA. I had no plan to talk of this tonight—

SCHAEFER. You're joking, right?

EZRA. It is best that such questions are not discussed in public.

SCHAEFER. I agree with you, Ezra, but there's five hundred people in there with one question on their minds. What is Israel going to do about this?

EZRA. Israel is fully cooperating with the United States authorities.

SCHAEFER. So tell them that. Because it's not only our own people. You've got all the reporters in there, and TV crews. You think they're here to film a bunch of Jews eating dinner?

EZRA. They do this?

SCHAEFER. Ezra, how many years do we know each other, you still haven't figured out my sense of humor?

EZRA. I am sorry, Arthur—

SCHAEFER. The only way to get this off the six o'clock news is to go in there and answer all their questions. (*Pause.*)

EZRA. It does not help that David Klein's wife is on television criticizing Israel ...

SCHAEFER. I saw that.

EZRA. Someone should speak with her.

SCHAEFER. (*Pause.*) Don't look at me—

EZRA. You were Sam Klein's closest friend.

SCHAEFER. I haven't spoken to them in years. When I heard it was David who was spying for you—

EZRA. Arthur, he did this on his own completely.

SCHAEFER. The point is, he's not some stranger. We can't say this is just another crackpot American kid who wanted to be famous for a few days. This is Sam Klein's son. You know what Sam did for Israel, the millions of dollars he raised ...

EZRA. I knew Sam Klein.

SCHAEFER. Everybody did.

EZRA. But no one so well as you ...

SCHAEFER. Which I guess is why every Jew in America is calling me for answers, like I'm the pope.

EZRA. You are one of their leaders ...

SCHAEFER. How are you explaining it, in Washington?

EZRA. You know the first rule of international relations? When things go wrong, blame the ambassador.

SCHAEFER. I think if I had to chose right now, I'd rather be pope.

EZRA. (*Pause.*) Arthur, you will speak to them?

SCHAEFER. Who?

EZRA. The Kleins. Explain to them how it is not helping anyone to make such statements in public.

SCHAEFER. I really wish you would find someone else.

EZRA. No one else understands the importance of private efforts. You said yourself, the rest do not stop talking.

SCHAEFER. I'm sure there's at least one other Jew in America who knows how to be a little quiet ...

EZRA. No one else can be so convincing as you.

SCHAEFER. I always agree with flattery. But this time you're wrong.

EZRA. Arthur, we all must do everything we can, even things that are not pleasant. Just as you want me to answer questions tonight—

SCHAEFER. What is this, Ezra, some kind of deal?

EZRA. I am asking you to help Israel, as you always do.

SCHAEFER. (*Pause*.) You really owe me for this one.

EZRA. Owe you what?

SCHAEFER. Lunch.

EZRA. You are saying you will go?

SCHAEFER. Are you giving me a choice?

(*SCHAEFER tries to lead EZRA into the ballroom, but HE doesn't move*.)

EZRA. And Arthur, perhaps while you are there, David Klein will tell you what he is saying to the prosecutors ...

SCHAEFER. You don't know?

EZRA. Israel is a foreign government. The U.S. Justice Department does not inform us.

SCHAEFER. What could David tell them? He walked out with those plans and brought them to you ...

EZRA. Sometimes, in such a situation, it is not uncommon, a man will feel isolated. He tells stories to the prosecutors, to win their friendship. You must tell him that Israel stands with him. We know he did this for the Jewish people.

(*There is a burst of NOISE from the ballroom*.)

SCHAEFER. Well we better go inside, before the Jewish people start a food riot ...

EZRA. They will do this?

SCHAEFER. I'm joking, Ezra.

EZRA. (*Smiling*.) I know. I also joke.

(*EZRA exits. The noise fades as SCHAEFER goes downstage. LIGHTS to black except for a SPOT on Schaefer.*)

Scene 4

SCHAEFER. (*Speaks to the audience.*) In the old days in Europe, they used to say, a Jew is someone with a Jewish sense of humor. Now today, for the first time in two thousand years, we have a Jewish country, and if you've been to Israel you know, they have the greatest soldiers in the world, but not one person with a Jewish sense of humor. You may have guessed by now, my original ambition was to be a comedian. (*Pause.*) Or maybe you haven't guessed, it was right after the war, I was maybe twenty, twenty-one, I did some standup in the Catskills. Not the big hotels, the bungalow colonies, the rooming houses ... the bottom of the show business ladder. Sam Klein was the one who made me realize that after the war, and the Six Million, there was more to do in life than making people laugh. "In these days of danger and catastrophe," he would say, "the Jews are constantly in peril. We have to act on a global scale, get all tangled up in major world questions on a daily basis." It was a full-time job. Sam convinced me I could do it.

(*HELEN and DAVID sit in the living room, reading newspapers.*)

SCHAEFER. And when I ran out of money my last year in the seminary, he paid my way. That was the kind of man that Sam Klein was, to the day he died.

(*LIGHTS DOWN on Schaefer.*)

Scene 5

LIGHTS come up on the Kleins' living room. Classical MUSIC is playing. There is a plaque on the wall. After watching a moment, SCHAEFER exits.

DAVID. .... listen to this, Mom. They had a dinner last night in York ...(*Reading:*) "...after his prepared speech, the ambassador was asked if he thought the incident would jeopardize the position of American Jews, perhaps bringing new accusations of 'dual loyalty.'" That's what they're worried about ...
HELEN. All they ever worry about is themselves ...
DAVID. (*Goes back to the paper.*) "On his way out of the hotel, the ambassador—"
RACHEL. (*Enters.*) David? I thought we were going for a walk?

DAVID. I just want to finish this article ...

RACHEL. I was waiting for you out back ...

DAVID. I didn't realize, I'm sorry. (*Stands.*)

HELEN. David, we're in the middle of a discussion.

DAVID. I just want to get some fresh air.

RACHEL. And it'll be dark soon ...

DAVID. Why don't you come with us, Mom?

RACHEL. She has her symphony board reception.

HELEN. But I'd like to finish our discussion...

DAVID. We will, when I get back—

HELEN. I'll be gone.

DAVID. So when you come home ...

HELEN. There's a meeting after the reception. I'll be late.

DAVID. I'll be up ...

RACHEL. David, your jacket's out by the door.

(*The DOORBELL chimes.*)

DAVID. Who's that?

HELEN. I'm not expecting anyone. (*To offstage:*) Who is it?

SCHAEFER. (*Offstage.*) Arthur Schaefer.

DAVID. Schaefer?

RACHEL. (*Pause.*) He called this morning and said he was in town, he might drop by ...

HELEN. And you invited him?

RACHEL. He wants to talk to David.

HELEN. I'd appreciate some notice when I'm having guests in my home.

RACHEL. I didn't think you'd be here ...

HELEN. That's a fine excuse ...

(*DAVID starts offstage.*)

RACHEL. David, where are you going?

DAVID. For a walk.

RACHEL. But the rabbi wants to talk to you.

DAVID. I don't want to talk to him.

HELEN. You can't leave, David.

(*RACHEL exits to let Schaefer in.*)

DAVID. Mom, you feel the same way about him as I do.

HELEN. Yes I do. But we have to be civil.

DAVID. Civil—?

(*RACHEL returns with SCHAEFER.*)

SCHAEFER. Helen. It's so good to see you...

HELEN. This is quite a surprise.

SCHAEFER. I called this morning, I told Rachel I was coming.

HELEN. She didn't mention it.

SCHAEFER. Is it a bad time?

HELEN. I've got an appointment in the city, I'll be leaving shortly—

RACHEL. David and I aren't going anywhere.

HELEN. (*Pause*.) Can I get you anything before I leave?

SCHAEFER. I'd love a coffee.

HELEN. (*Pause*.) Yes. Of course. I'll just be a moment. (*Exits*.)

SCHAEFER. It's good to see you, David.

DAVID. Good to see you.

SCHAEFER. (*Shaking David's hand*.) It's been a long time.

DAVID. Yes it has.

SCHAEFER. I don't have to tell you I've been thinking about you a lot.

DAVID. Thank you.

SCHAEFER. I know this is difficult for you.

DAVID. It's okay ...

SCHAEFER. You know we're doing everything we can to help you.

DAVID. All I've heard is people saying I'm a Jewish traitor ...

SCHAEFER. That's why these things are always better handled quietly, behind the scenes. Talking about it in public makes it harder on everyone.

DAVID. I suppose so.

SCHAEFER. You might want to keep that in mind yourselves.

DAVID. Excuse me?

SCHAEFER. I saw Rachel on TV the other night. It doesn't help the situation ...

DAVID. Is that why you're here?

SCHAEFER. I'm here because your father was my closest friend.

DAVID. But we don't hear a word from you until you don't like what we say on television?

SCHAEFER. I was shocked when I first heard, we all were—

DAVID. (*Picking up newspaper.*) Not too shocked to issue condemnations on the spot, before you could be accused of "dual loyalty"—

SCHAEFER. The newspapers don't tell you everything that's in people's hearts—

DAVID. They tell you when people don't care.

SCHAEFER. Of course we care—

DAVID. About yourselves. About "dual loyalty"—

RACHEL. David, don't talk like that.

SCHAEFER. It's all right, really, I never mind hearing an opinion.

HELEN. (*Enters with a cup of coffee, milk and sugar on a tray.*) How do you take your coffee, Rabbi?

SCHAEFER. Black. And it's Arthur, you know that.

HELEN. I'd forgotten. (*Long pause. HELEN pours his coffee.*)

SCHAEFER. I can see nobody is thrilled to see me here. I know I owe you all an apology, that I haven't been in closer touch ...

HELEN. It isn't necessary.

SCHAEFER. And I should've been here the very first day I heard this news, to see if I could help—

DAVID. We don't need any help. I did what I thought was right, and I'm prepared to pay the price.

SCHAEFER. No one doubts your idealism, David, or your love for Israel. We have a question or two about your methods ...

DAVID. (*Pointing at the plaque.*) You see that plaque on the wall? My father got it in 1948—

SCHAEFER. I have the same plaque—

DAVID. For helping Israel get weapons to defend itself against the Arabs. You were heroes. When I do the same thing—

SCHAEFER. It's not the same—

DAVID. No it isn't. You got a plaque, I get called a traitor ...

SCHAEFER. We just wonder why you had to do this on your own, without talking to someone first?

HELEN. Like you?

SCHAEFER. Like anyone who could explain the consequences—

DAVID. You want to talk about consequences, Rabbi? There are Soviet missiles in Syria right now that can reach Jerusalem or Tel Aviv in minutes. The only defense against them is a system developed by the U.S. Air Force. Our government refused to let Israel have the system. So I got it for them.

SCHAEFER. There are other ways to accomplish things—

DAVID. You're right, you're right, the United States has a written agreement to share defense technology with Israel, but they refused to keep that agreement. Just like they refused to bomb the railroad lines to Auschwitz when that also would have saved Jewish lives. I just did what I had to do.

SCHAEFER. You didn't have to make the decision by yourself—

DAVID. It was an easy decision. I was always told to put the Jewish people ahead of myself, my father always told me that. So did you.

SCHAEFER. We never told you to break the law—

DAVID. (*Pointing at the plaque.*) Was running guns legal in 1948?

SCHAEFER. David, I didn't come here to argue with you—

DAVID. Why did you come here?

SCHAEFER. I told you, to help—

DAVID. And I told you, we don't need your help.

RACHEL. David—

DAVID. I thought we were going for a walk? (*Exits.*)

RACHEL. David—! (*Exits after David.*)

HELEN. (*To Schaefer.*) Well, thank you for coming, Rabbi. I know you went out of your way.

SCHAEFER. Helen, give me a chance to explain—

HELEN. There's nothing to explain.

SCHAEFER. I know I remind you that Sam is gone—

HELEN. You remind me of why he's gone.

SCHAEFER. It was an accident.

HELEN. If you hadn't taken him to Israel, there would've been no accident.

SCHAEFER. It was important—

HELEN. It was always important. Every time you disrupted this family, dragged him to a meeting, took him on some mission, it was always important—

SCHAEFER. A traffic accident could happen anywhere—

(*RACHEL enters.*)

HELEN. But it happened there. And after all he did, all the money he gave, the time he spent, his life, they let his son be arrested in front of their embassy.

SCHAEFER. They had no choice—

HELEN. Then why did they tell him to come there?

SCHAEFER. Who told him?

RACHEL. (*Pause.*) Ephraim did.

SCHAEFER. Who's Ephraim?

RACHEL. The one who took the plans. He said, if David ever felt he was in any danger, he'd be safe at the embassy.

SCHAEFER. He had no right, he doesn't work for the government—

HELEN. He has an office in the embassy.

SCHAEFER. What office?

RACHEL. On the second floor, that's where David met him ...

SCHAEFER. No one in authority in Israel had the slightest idea he was dealing with David.

HELEN. But they're willing to use what he brought them. They're willing to build the defense system. The only thing they aren't willing to do is help the person who got it for them ...

(*A mantelpiece CLOCK chimes.*)

HELEN. I'm sorry. I'm late.

SCHAEFER. Helen, this is important—

HELEN. So is my appointment. Rachel will show you out. (*Exits.*)

SCHAEFER. (*Pause.*) I guess I upset them ...

RACHEL. They were upset before you came.

SCHAEFER. Rachel, you have to believe me, there are a lot of people trying to help, in Washington, and in Israel—

RACHEL. What are they doing?

SCHAEFER. I don't know all the details myself—

RACHEL. Could you find out? (*Pause.*) You said you wanted to help.

SCHAEFER. I get the feeling David doesn't want my help.

RACHEL. He's just worried. The sentencing isn't for another six weeks. His lawyers don't think they'll be hard on him, it's not like he spied for Russia or anything ...

SCHAEFER. I don't understand, the lawyers "think"? Didn't they negotiate a sentence before he pleaded guilty?

RACHEL. David said he didn't do anything wrong and he wouldn't plea-bargain like a criminal.

SCHAEFER. He's a very determined young man.

RACHEL. (*Going to him.*) Helen would kill me if she knew I was asking you, that I was talking to you this way ...

SCHAEFER. She'll never know. There's an old Jewish saying. The reason Adam and Eve lived nine hundred years is that neither one of them had a mother-in-law.

RACHEL. I just want to know what's going on ... And David's father always said that you know everyone.

SCHAEFER. I know a few people ... I've never had much to do with the Justice Department...

RACHEL. Whatever you could find out, Rabbi, is more than we know now ...

SCHAEFER. (*Pause.*) I'll be in Washington the day after tomorrow. I'll call Congressman Fitzgerald, he's an old friend. I'll see what I can dig up ...

RACHEL. I don't know how to thank you ...

SCHAEFER. (*Smiling.*) Can I make a suggestion?

RACHEL. What?

SCHAEFER. Don't call any press conferences till you hear from me?

RACHEL. (*Smiling.*) I promise.

SCHAEFER. Well, the Metroliner doesn't wait for rabbis. Say goodbye to David?

RACHEL. I will.

SCHAEFER. And Helen. If she'll hear it.

(*SCHAEFER kisses her goodbye and exits. After a moment, DAVID enters zipping his jacket.*)

DAVID. He's gone?

RACHEL. I don't think you're being fair to him, David—

DAVID. I thought we were going for a walk?

RACHEL. He really cares about you—

DAVID. All he cares about is "dual loyalty"...

RACHEL. Then why is he going to speak to his friends in Washington about your case?

DAVID. What "friends"?

RACHEL. You know he has all kinds of high-level connections—

DAVID. Did you tell him we don't want anything from him or his "connections"?

RACHEL. I told him we would appreciate anything he could do to help ...

DAVID. Why?

RACHEL. What's wrong with giving him a chance—?

DAVID. He's had plenty of chances.

RACHEL. Maybe he can help—

DAVID. He can't help.

RACHEL. How do you know that—?

DAVID. I know.

RACHEL. Well I don't see how it hurts—

DAVID. (*Shouting at her, furious.*) Why won't you listen to me? He can't help!

RACHEL. (*Pause. Walks away from him.*) You don't have to shout at me like that ...

DAVID. I'm not—

RACHEL. You never used to shout at me like that.

DAVID. I'm sorry.

RACHEL. (*Pause.*) I just wish none of this had ever happened ...

DAVID. So do I.

RACHEL. And we were back home, in our own home.

DAVID. You know the reporters wouldn't let us live in Washington—

RACHEL. She doesn't let us live here! I'm tired of spending all my time with someone who hates me—

DAVID. My mother likes you—

RACHEL. David, please.

DAVID. She's just not herself right now—

RACHEL. Oh yes she is.

DAVID. It'll just be a little while longer. They'll find a sex scandal or something and forget all about me ... Then we'll be able to go home ... (*HE puts his arms around her.*) It'll just be the two of us, just like before, I promise ... (*Pause.*) Until I have to go away.

RACHEL. David!

(*SHE puts her arms around him. LIGHTS fade except for a SPOT on Schaefer as HE enters downstage.*)

Scene 6

SCHAEFER. (*Speaks to the audience.*) Some rabbis say it isn't for a Jew to ask questions at all, just obey the Law of God.

(*DAVID and RACHEL exit.*)

SCHAEFER. But what the Law is, how we know what to obey, this is something Jews have argued about since we got the Law. Is it the Torah? Is it the Talmud? Is it history itself, or the necessities of survival? You could say, a Jew is a person involved in this argument about the Law. Or any other argument, for that matter. Take Moshe Rabbenu, Moses the law-giver himself. The first time God calls to him in Sinai, he goes up on the mountain, and God says, "Go back to Egypt, and tell Pharaoh to let the Jews out." And what does Moses do? He argues, with God no less. "You have to be kidding. I am slow of speech and slow of tongue. Go get somebody else."

(*FITZGERALD enters and sits down in Whitney's office.*)

SCHAEFER. Which is what I should've said to Ezra in the first place ... (*Turns to Fitzgerald.*)

Scene 7

LIGHTS UP on an office in the Justice Department. Offstage, TYPEWRITERS and TELEPHONES can be heard.

SCHAEFER. So tell me what this guy is like.

FITZGERALD. Deputy Assistant Attorney General Wingate P. Whitney? What does he sound like he'd be like?

SCHAEFER. Not somebody who makes a career in the Justice Department.

FITZGERALD. Win is actually a classic example of American family values, Arthur. The only people who think he's of any value are his family.

SCHAEFER. Why do they put someone like that on a case like this?

FITZGERALD. No one else in Washington would get within a mile of it. It takes a Wingate P. Whitney to see Israel-bashing as a career opportunity.

SCHAEFER. That isn't the best news you ever gave me, Frank ...

FITZGERALD. It's why I thought I'd come along. Besides, I owe it to Sam. He helped me finance every one of my campaigns, God rest his soul. When I heard this was David ... Helen must be devastated.

HELEN. She seems to be holding up okay ...

FITZGERALD. Well, it's good you're getting involved, Arthur. We really need to put this thing to rest. Whitney's not the only anti-semite falling out of the cherry trees in this town.

SCHAEFER. (*Pause.*) Ezra told me ...

FITZGERALD. I'm happy he's aware of it.

SCHAEFER. Of course he is.

FITZGERALD. Then why doesn't he return my phone calls?

SCHAEFER. You know he's very busy with all this ...

FITZGERALD. Arthur, we're supposed to be on the same side. With Ezra these days, I get the feeling he thinks I'm the enemy.

SCHAEFER. (*Pause. Motioning at the desk.*) So where is he already?

FITZGERALD. With this guy, who knows. But I bet he tells us he was in a very important meeting with the "A-G."

SCHAEFER. Who?

FITZGERALD. The Attorney General.

SCHAEFER. I can't believe he keeps you waiting like this.

FITZGERALD. I'm just a congressman, Arthur. This is a permanent civil servant.

WHITNEY. (*Enters, holding a pile of phone messages.*) Gentlemen, sorry to keep you waiting. I was briefing the A-G.

FITZGERALD. Win, you know Rabbi Schaefer?

WHITNEY. Only by reputation. A pleasure, Rabbi.

(*THEY shake hands.*)

WHITNEY. Well, gentlemen, what can the Department of Justice do for you?

SCHAEFER. We're interested in the David Klein case, Mr. Whitney ...

FITZGERALD. And who isn't, these days? I've never seen so much press when there isn't even the slightest hint of sexual perversion.

WHITNEY. Espionage is sensational enough, Congressman.

FITZGERALD. Now let's not be calling it espionage, what with two friendly governments involved.

WHITNEY. What would you call it?

SCHAEFER. There's an old Jewish joke about a spy—

WHITNEY. Rabbi, I'm a bit pressed for time.

FITZGERALD. Win—

SCHAEFER. You're right, Mr. Whitney, we should get right to the point and not waste your valuable time.

WHITNEY. I appreciate it.

SCHAEFER. We just want to know where the case stands ...

WHITNEY. David Klein pleaded guilty to espionage. He'll be sentenced next month.

SCHAEFER. We were wondering what sentence you plan to recommend to the judge?

WHITNEY. We intend to recommend the maximum. Life in prison.

SCHAEFER. The maximum—

WHITNEY. We have no reason not to.

SCHAEFER. But David was acting out of idealism. And he's never done anything wrong. Don't you think that life in prison is a little severe?

WHITNEY. There are people in this government, Rabbi Schaefer, who don't think life in prison is nearly severe enough for David Klein.

FITZGERALD. There are also people in this government who think we should've given those plans to Israel in the first place.

WHITNEY. Are you prepared to justify the transfer of secret American military information to a foreign power?

FITZGERALD. If I justify it, which I certainly don't need to do to you, it's because Israel is a major asset to our national security—

WHITNEY. That's outside my area of expertise—

FITZGERALD. You don't have to remind us.

SCHAEFER. Mr. Whitney, there must be some way that we can avoid a very unpleasant public controversy over this sentence. (*Pause.*)

WHITNEY. Are you trying to threaten me, Rabbi?

SCHAEFER. Of course not—

FITZGERALD. Why don't you tell us what you want from the boy?

WHITNEY. What we want is his full and faithful testimony. How he got access to the plans, how he removed them from the Pentagon computers. How long the operation went on. I'm sure even you understand the importance of that for our "national security."

SCHAEFER. What "operation?" David just took those plans and gave them to this Israeli ...

WHITNEY. That's one theory.

SCHAEFER. I don't understand ...

WHITNEY. There is another theory. That David Klein was recruited by Israeli intelligence—

SCHAEFER. That's not true!

WHITNEY. And his superiors have ordered him to take all the blame himself, in order to protect their other operations.

SCHAEFER. There are no other operations! Israel doesn't spy on the United States—

WHITNEY. All nations spy on one another ...

FITZGERALD. You're reading too many novels, Win.

SCHAEFER. Mr. Whitney, surely you don't believe this "other theory"?

WHITNEY. We have no evidence to refute it.

SCHAEFER. What about the person who got the documents, can't he tell you?

WHITNEY. Our best information is that he returned to Israel a few hours after David Klein was arrested. And the government of Israel claims they don't know where he is, or even who he is...

FITZGERALD. So you're saying he's the one you need?

WHITNEY. I'm saying that if we were given all the facts by both these men, we would be able to re-evaluate our interpretation of this case, and frame our recommendation to the court accordingly. (*HE looks at his watch.*) I'm sorry, gentlemen, but I must run— (*Starts out.*)

SCHAEFER. Mr. Whitney. This is more than a criminal case. It affects the strategic relationship between the United States and Israel, which has been of enormous benefit to both countries, to both peoples, for four decades. This case has tremendous political implications—

WHITNEY. It's not my job to worry about political implications.

FITZGERALD. Espionage is a political crime, what kind of implications do you expect?

WHITNEY. We expect cooperation. (*Looks at his watch.*) Now gentlemen, I really must go. It was a pleasure to meet you, Rabbi Schaefer. I look forward to your help with this problem. Congressman. (*Exits.*)

SCHAEFER. Why does everyone I meet these days ask me for help?

FITZGERALD. (*Putting his hand on Schaefer's shoulder.*) I warned you about him, didn't I?

SCHAEFER. Well, I guess the next thing is, we better talk to Ezra ...

FITZGERALD. (*Nodding, but moving away.*) I wonder if it wouldn't be less awkward for you to talk with him alone? Keep it in the family, so to speak?

SCHAEFER. You are family, Frank—

FITZGERALD. I appreciate that, I appreciate that, but I suspect you'll get much farther without me there. (*Pause.*)

SCHAEFER. Maybe I will ...

FITZGERALD. I'm sure you will. Let's go, Arthur ... (*Exits.*)

(*LIGHTS fade.*)

Scene 8

LIGHTS UP on the cafeteria in the Israeli Embassy. Offstage, KITCHEN SOUNDS. An EMPLOYEE sets up a table as EZRA enters carrying a tray.

SCHAEFER. ... I couldn't believe this Whitney, Ezra. Ice cubes wouldn't melt in his mouth.

(*The EMPLOYEE exits. EZRA and SCHAEFER sit at the table. EZRA eats steadily and heartily. SCHAEFER barely picks at his food.*

EZRA. He is no friend of Israel.

SCHAEFER. Who knows if he even has a friend? But he's not inventing this, he's got the go-ahead from higher up.

EZRA. There are unfortunately many officials of the U.S. government wishing to sabotage the friendship of Israel and America. And also the position of American Jews.

SCHAEFER. All he did was complain, David won't cooperate, you won't ...

EZRA. I have told you, Arthur, we are fully cooperating.

SCHAEFER. Whitney said you won't even admit you know who Ephraim is.

EZRA. Who is Ephraim?

SCHAEFER. Ezra, the Kleins told me his name—

EZRA. Who is he?

SCHAEFER. The fellow who got the plans from David. They said he worked in your embassy—

EZRA. This embassy has no such an employee.

SCHAEFER. They said he had an office on the second floor—

EZRA. This cannot be so.

SCHAEFER. And Whitney thinks he's an intelligence agent.

EZRA. Arthur, the United States is a friendly country with a large Jewish population. The State of Israel would not have agents here.

SCHAEFER. I told him that. But they want us to prove it, or they're going to put David in jail for the rest of his life.

EZRA. I do not think so ...

SCHAEFER. They figure, if David looks at life in prison, he might have a few more things to say ...

EZRA. (*Pause.*) Do you think so?

SCHAEFER. What?

EZRA. That David Klein will tell them anything?

SCHAEFER. It won't be easy to convince him, but it's the only way to get him off. Frank and I both got the same message. All they want from David is how he got through their security. It's this Ephraim they're really after.

EZRA. You believe this, Arthur?

SCHAEFER. They want out from under this as much as we do, that's why they're willing to deal. We just have to get this Ephraim to testify.

EZRA. Even if this man is found to be in Israel, we cannot simply order a private citizen to testify against himself.

SCHAEFER. You have laws against private citizens interfering in foreign policy. Arrest him, let the Justice Department extradite him—

EZRA. It is not so simple.

SCHAEFER. He's the one responsible. Why do you want to protect him?

EZRA. No one is protecting him.

SCHAEFER. If you don't produce him, David's going to jail for life, and Whitney's going to tell the world that he was a regular agent who's covering up for you.

EZRA. It isn't true—

SCHAEFER. But it'll sound a lot more believable on the six o'clock news.

EZRA. (*Pause.*) I will tell this to Jerusalem ...

SCHAEFER. Tell them this thing is already starting to hurt us. Even Frank Fitzgerald, an absolute friend of ours, is getting nervous. He ducked this lunch ...

EZRA. I did not know Frank to be a coward.

SCHAEFER. He's a politician, with that built-in radar, he gets within ten miles of a problem all his bells go off. And if Frank Fitzgerald is feeling the heat, how many people are getting ready to bail out on us completely? (*Looks at his watch and stands.*) I want to catch the two o'clock train, stop off in Philly and see the Kleins ...

EZRA. Do not give them false hope, Arthur.

SCHAEFER. What's false about it?

EZRA. (*Pause.*) Arthur, you didn't eat your lunch ...

SCHAEFER. I'm not hungry.

EZRA. You really should eat ...

SCHAEFER. You want me to eat? Next time you pay off a lunch debt, take me somewhere besides your cafeteria. (*Exits.*)

(*EZRA moves Schaefer's plate in front of him and continues eating. BLACKOUT.*)

Scene 9

LIGHTS UP on the Kleins' living room. There is a tea service, and a copy of <u>Fear No Evil</u> by Natan Sharansky on a table. The mantelpiece CLOCK ticks in the background. The DOORBELL chimes.
HELEN enters from inside the house. SCHAEFER enters from outside.

SCHAEFER. Hello, Helen.
HELEN. You're here again?
SCHAEFER. I tried to call from Washington, and when I got here, but your line was busy ... Is it a bad time?
HELEN. Yes.
SCHAEFER. I have some news for David—
HELEN. Why don't you leave me your telephone number and I'll tell him you were here?
SCHAEFER. Is Rachel here?
HELEN. No.
SCHAEFER. Well, I have a dinner tonight in New York, but I can afford to be a little late. (*HE points to tea service.*) Is that coffee?
HELEN. Tea.
SCHAEFER. I could use a cup of tea, the train really shook up my stomach ... (*Pause.*)
HELEN. Do sit down. (*Pours a cup of tea for him.*)
SCHAEFER. I don't remember Sam being much of a tea drinker ...

HELEN. He wasn't. Why do you want to see David?

SCHAEFER. (*Spots the book and picks it up.*) Who's reading Sharansky's book?

HELEN. David is.

SCHAEFER. I had the honor to meet him my last trip to Israel. A true hero. There aren't many of those left ...

HELEN. You didn't answer me—

SCHAEFER. (*Pointing to the cup in her hand.*) Is that mine?

(*HELEN hands HIM the cup of tea and HE sips it.*)

SCHAEFER. Delicious ...

HELEN. Rabbi Schaefer—

SCHAEFER. Arthur, please.

HELEN. Will you please tell me why you're here?

SCHAEFER. Do you know what Reb Nachman of Bratzlav used to say? It was so hard for Satan to mislead the world all by himself, he had to appoint prominent rabbis in different localities to assist him.

(*DAVID and RACHEL enter. THEY see Schaefer and stop.*)

DAVID. What are you doing here?

SCHAEFER. I have some news for you—

RACHEL. What news?

DAVID. I don't need any news from you—

SCHAEFER. Congressman Fitzgerald and I had a meeting with Wingate Whitney—

HELEN. Why are you talking to him?

SCHAEFER. About David's legal situation.

DAVID. Since when are you a lawyer?

SCHAEFER. I'm trying to be a friend.

RACHEL. What did he say, Rabbi?

DAVID. It doesn't matter what he said—

SCHAEFER. The government, our government, is ready to make a deal—

DAVID. I'm not interested.

SCHAEFER. Why are you so stubborn?

DAVID. Why are you so pushy?

SCHAEFER. I just want to help—

DAVID. Well I want you to leave, you're upsetting my family.

SCHAEFER. They'll be more upset when you go to prison for the rest of your life.

HELEN. What—?

RACHEL. His life?

SCHAEFER. Whitney told us he's going to recommend the maximum sentence—

HELEN. Why?

DAVID. That's not what my lawyers say—

SCHAEFER. They weren't there.

RACHEL. How can they do that?

SCHAEFER. Whitney is taking the position that David was a regular agent, working for Israel ongoing—

DAVID. Israel doesn't use Jews to spy on their own countries.

SCHAEFER. I told him that. He wouldn't take my word for it.

HELEN. Why should he?

SCHAEFER. But he also said they'll change their position if you agree to cooperate—

RACHEL. Cooperate how?

DAVID. Rachel, stay out of this—

RACHEL. "Stay out" of it ...?

SCHAEFER. They just want you to tell them how you got through their security.

DAVID. How does that prove to them I'm not an agent?

SCHAEFER. That part will come from Ephraim ... (*Pause.*)

DAVID. Ephraim ...? (*Pause.*)

RACHEL. I told him, David.

DAVID. Why did you do that?

SCHAEFER. There's no reason to protect him. He's the one who caused the whole fiasco, posing as an intelligence officer ...

RACHEL. He wasn't posing.

DAVID. Stop it, Rachel—

RACHEL. You told me you checked him out—

SCHAEFER. I don't understand—

DAVID. Neither does she.

RACHEL. You told me you checked him out!

DAVID. I just made sure he was with intelligence, that's all.

SCHAEFER. He's not.

DAVID. You think I would risk my life passing secret information to someone who wouldn't know what to do with it?

SCHAEFER. That's not how I understand it—

DAVID. Then you don't understand it.

SCHAEFER. (*Pause.*) Well, the important thing is they're willing to compromise—

DAVID. But they want more than my cooperation. They want me to give them somebody else—

SCHAEFER. Israel is going to do that, not you—

RACHEL. They said they will?

DAVID. They won't. I won't be part of it. I will not betray another Jew to save myself.

SCHAEFER. That's not what this is—

DAVID. That's exactly what it is.

SCHAEFER. If Whitney says publicly that you were recruited by Israeli intelligence—

DAVID. I wasn't recruited!

SCHAEFER. That's what we have to prove.

DAVID. I'm telling you for the last time. I won't be part of any deal. Do you understand me?

SCHAEFER. Yes. You want some time to think it over.

DAVID. Is that some kind of joke?

SCHAEFER. David, this is your decision—

DAVID. I'm glad you realize that—

SCHAEFER. But I want you to change your mind.

DAVID. (*Pause.*) I will not change my mind. Believe me.

(*SCHAEFER turns to Helen.*)

HELEN. You heard my son.

SCHAEFER. (*To David.*) Will you call me if you do?

DAVID. Goodbye, Rabbi Schaefer.

SCHAEFER. (*Pause.*) I'm sorry, Rachel. (*Exits.*)

DAVID. Do you believe that old windbag? (*Picks up his book.*)

HELEN. Let's hope that's the last we'll see of him.

RACHEL. He's the only one who wants to help us—

HELEN. He just want us to think he's the most important man in the world, he always did.

RACHEL. Didn't you hear a word he said?

HELEN. I heard—

RACHEL. Don't you care?

HELEN. I care—

RACHEL. Am I the only one who cares?

DAVID. Of course we care.

RACHEL. Why are you being so stubborn?

DAVID. I didn't do anything wrong—

RACHEL. That doesn't matter—

DAVID. It matters to me! It obviously doesn't matter to you. (*Sits down to read.*)

RACHEL. David, the only thing that matters to me is being with you.

DAVID. We will be—

RACHEL. When? You heard what he said—

DAVID. He doesn't know what he's talking about—

RACHEL. He knows, David—

DAVID. He doesn't know a thing.

RACHEL. He knows a lot more than you do!

DAVID. (*Purposefully.*) He doesn't know a thing.

(*Long pause. DAVID opens his book and reads. RACHEL stares at him.*)

RACHEL. Oh my God ...

DAVID. What?

RACHEL. It's true ...

DAVID. What's true?

RACHEL. They recruited you ...

DAVID. Of course not.

RACHEL. That's why you're protecting them.

DAVID. I'm not—

RACHEL. What did they make you do, David, take an oath?

DAVID. Of course not—

RACHEL. Don't lie to me—

DAVID. I'm not lying—

RACHEL. I have a right to know the truth!

DAVID. (*Pause.*) They didn't make me take any oath—

HELEN. David! What are you saying?

DAVID. He didn't "recruit" me. He knew who I was, that I had security clearance—

HELEN. Oh David no ...

DAVID. He told me they needed the system, the United States was leaving them defenseless. So I got it for them. That doesn't make me an "agent" ...

HELEN. David, you lied to me—
RACHEL. He lied to everyone.
HELEN. And all this time I've defended you—
DAVID. Mom—
HELEN. Everywhere I've gone since this awful thing happened I've been asked and I've explained that you're an idealist and you did what you thought was right. As much as I hate what you did, and what it's done to all of us, I defended you, David, because I believed in you, in your integrity. And now you tell me you were lying?
DAVID. I didn't lie—
HELEN. I'll never forgive you for this, David. Never!
DAVID. Mom—!

(*HELEN exits.*)

DAVID. She's so upset ... I never saw her so upset ... Even when my father died, the worst thing ever happened in her life ...
RACHEL. I don't blame her.
DAVID. Rachel, I didn't lie to you. There were things I didn't tell you—
RACHEL. What's the difference?
DAVID. If I told you you'd be part of it, they'd be trying to put you in jail too. I didn't want to hurt you—
RACHEL. Oh you think you didn't hurt me?
DAVID. I never meant to ...

RACHEL. You know what hurts the most? You always said I was the most important thing in your life—

DAVID. You are—

RACHEL. But they're more important, aren't they?

DAVID. No—

RACHEL. And I stood by you, they locked their door in your face—

DAVID. They had to—

RACHEL. It's a door, it opens—

DAVID. You heard Schaefer, if people think they recruited an American Jew, what the reaction would be!

RACHEL. I thought he was just an old windbag?

DAVID. (*Pause.*) It doesn't matter who initiated it. I thought it was the right thing to do. I was always taught to put the Jewish people ahead of myself—

RACHEL. By your father.

DAVID. You can't expect me to betray my whole life—

RACHEL. It is not just your life, David! It is my life too—

DAVID. I know that—

RACHEL. I trusted you! Even when the FBI was banging on our door, and you were dragging me out the back, telling me you're a spy, and I should get down on the floor of the car in case they started shooting ... David, shooting!

DAVID. I know ...

RACHEL. I trusted you. That you would never do anything to hurt me—

DAVID. I wouldn't—

RACHEL. And I've never told you what to do, you know that. I've never been that kind of wife, I didn't want to be, I didn't think you needed my advice, a brilliant man like you—

DAVID. I'm not a brilliant man—

RACHEL. But now I'm telling you, David. You have to make a deal with them.

DAVID. I can't—

RACHEL. You don't have to tell them you were recruited, all they want to know is how you got through their security—

DAVID. That's not all they want—

RACHEL. That's what they told the rabbi—

DAVID. But once my lawyers start to plea bargain, they'll just get tougher and tougher—

RACHEL. So don't have the lawyers to do it, let Rabbi Schaefer go back to Whitney—

DAVID. It's the same thing! They'll still think I'm getting scared!

RACHEL. (*Pause.*) Aren't you getting scared? I'm getting scared. They want to put my husband in jail for the rest of his life ... and I'm scared ...

DAVID. It'll be all right—

RACHEL. It won't be all right. It won't be all right ...

DAVID. (*Looking at the plaque.*) You can't expect me to betray another Jew to save myself ...

RACHEL. David, I'm another Jew. Why are you betraying me?

DAVID. I'm not betraying you—

RACHEL. You promised to spend your life with me, remember? When we were married? Not in prison, with me. Don't I deserve some loyalty too?

DAVID. Of course you do ...

RACHEL. I don't want you to be in prison for the rest of your life ...

DAVID. I don't either—

RACHEL. I couldn't bear it. I love you, David. More than anything ...

DAVID. So do I ...

RACHEL. What?

DAVID. Love you ...

RACHEL. More than anything?

DAVID. Of course ...

RACHEL. Then you have to make a deal.

(*Long silence. THEY stare at each other. The mantelpiece CLOCK ticks loudly.*)

DAVID. All right.

RACHEL. What?

DAVID. I'll do it ...

RACHEL. You will?

DAVID. I'll make the deal ...

(*SHE throws her arms around him.*)

DAVID. Because I do, I love you more than anything ...

RACHEL. Oh David ...

DAVID. I wish to God I didn't ...

(*HE puts one arm around her. LIGHTS fade except for a SPOT on SCHAEFER as HE enters downstage.*)

Scene 10

SCHAEFER. (*Speaks to the audience.*) All the pieces fell into place in a hurry. David agreed to tell the Justice Department how he got the secrets out of the Pentagon. Israel agreed to let the Justice Department talk to Ephraim.

(*DAVID and RACHEL exit.*)

SCHAEFER. Well, they didn't agree just like that, it took a little bit of intercontinental arm-twisting. But they finally realized the only way to put this thing to rest was to tell the truth. As for David's sentence, we got it down to fifteen years, ten suspended, eligible for parole after two. Which I thought was fair. I've done a lot of deals in my time, but this one, with all the ramifications and strong emotions on every side, this one was the best. It reminded me of the first time I went back to Israel after the Six Day War. I went directly to Jerusalem, to the Old City, ours again after nineteen years. It was clogged with Jews, soldiers and hasidim and children and tourists, walking through the streets, praying together at the Wall. And there was a sense of pride, of accomplishment, you could practically touch it in the air. If you're old enough you remember that feeling, no matter what kind of Jew you are, no matter where you were when Jerusalem was freed. After two thousand years of powerlessness, the Jews went out and put their footprints on the world, instead of the other way around. You can grow to love that feeling. You can forget that all you are, after all, is just a Jew... (*Goes upstage.*)

Scene 11

LIGHTS up on the courtroom. The sound of VOICES in the background. HELEN, RACHEL and SCHAEFER take seats to one side, WHITNEY on the other. DAVID enters and stands downstage center, facing the audience.

JUDGE'S VOICE. David Klein, you are charged with three counts of espionage against the United States of America. You have pleaded guilty to all the charges against you, is that correct?
DAVID. Yes, your Honor.
JUDGE'S VOICE. Have you done so of your own free will?

DAVID. I have.

JUDGE'S VOICE. Have you done so free of pressure or threats of any kind?

DAVID. Yes, your Honor, I have.

JUDGE'S VOICE. Is there anything you wish to say to the court before your sentencing, Mr. Klein?

DAVID. There is, your honor.

JUDGE'S VOICE. You may do so at this time.

DAVID. Your honor, I never intended to harm the United States. I love this country and I've devoted my career to its defense. I have an equal love for Israel, your Honor, for the Jewish people. Their defense is just as important to me. There are those who say it isn't possible to love two countries at the same time, that there has to be a conflict of loyalties. They say my own case proves the proposition. But I say that Israel and the United States stand for the same ideals in the world, the same belief in freedom, and human dignity, and justice. As long as both countries continue to do so, there can be no conflict between them, or any conflict of loyalties for those of us who share those values. That's all I wanted to say.

JUDGE'S VOICE. Mr. Klein, I can see that you are a sincere and dedicated man. I also know that you have cooperated with the prosecutors, and such cooperation is taken into account by the court whenever a convicted criminal appears for sentencing. Of course the crime you have committed is not like other crimes. Treason is more heinous even than murder. Murder takes one life. Treason jeopardizes millions. In the opinion of this court, there can be no bargaining with treason. There can be no leniency ...

RACHEL. (*Softly.*) No ...

JUDGE'S VOICE. It is therefore the decision of this court that the defendant, David Klein, shall be sentenced to spend the rest of his natural days in prison—

RACHEL.	DAVID.
(*Screaming.*) No!	Rachel ...

JUDGE'S VOICE. With no possibility of parole— (*The sound of VOICES, rising.*) Sentence to begin immediately—

SCHAEFER.	RACHEL.
We had a deal!	You promised—

JUDGE'S VOICE. The defendant is remanded to the federal marshal, and court is dismissed. (*WHITNEY exits.*)

RACHEL. You promised! You promised! You promised ... (*BLACKOUT.*)

End of Act I

ACT II

Scene 1

MUSIC and the sound of VOICES. LIGHTS UP on the dining room of a private club. WHITNEY is eating lunch alone. SCHAEFER and FITZGERALD storm in, chased by the HEADWAITER.

HEADWAITER. Gentlemen, please you cannot come in here like this—

FITZGERALD. Whitney!

HEADWAITER. This is a private club—

WHITNEY. What is this—?

FITZGERALD. We have to talk to you—!

HEADWAITER. Mr. Whitney, I told them this was not allowed—

WHITNEY. I'll take care of it, Julian—

FITZGERALD. The way you took care of the sentence?

HEADWAITER. They've disrupted the entire club—

WHITNEY. It's all right, Julian, thank you. I'll take care of it.

HEADWAITER. Very well ... (*Exits.*)

WHITNEY. Now what do you think you're doing here?

FITZGERALD. We want to know why you gave him life—

WHITNEY. The judge did—

FITZGERALD. You were supposed to reduce the sentence—

SCHAEFER. And send him to a minimum-security prison. They're taking him to Petersburg—

WHITNEY. That's a federal facility, espionage is a federal crime—

SCHAEFER. That isn't what we agreed—

WHITNEY. What we agreed, Rabbi, was subject to the full cooperation of all the parties.

SCHAEFER. David told you everything he did—

WHITNEY. I'm talking about your Israeli friends.

SCHAEFER. They gave you Ephraim—

WHITNEY. Did they?

SCHAEFER. Wasn't he at the Embassy this morning—?

WHITNEY. No he wasn't.

FITZGERALD. What are you talking about?

WHITNEY. He never arrived.

FITZGERALD. He was supposed to—

WHITNEY. Yes. He was.

SCHAEFER. I'm sure he will—

WHITNEY. When?

SCHAEFER. (*Pause.*) I don't know ...

FITZGERALD. There must be some kind of mix-up ...

WHITNEY. The procedure was not that complicated.

SCHAEFER. That's why the judge sentenced David to life?

WHITNEY. The agreement wasn't honored—

SCHAEFER. It was by David! You can't blame him for some confusion in Israel—

WHITNEY. He was an agent of Israel.

FITZGERALD. I don't care if he's the reincarnation of Benedict Arnold. You had a deal, the boy kept his part and you didn't keep yours. This government cannot break its word to one of our own citizens!

WHITNEY. Don't try to intimidate me, Congressman Fitzgerald. This is a private club!

FITZGERALD. I'm not trying to intimidate you. I'll leave that to the million angry Jews who'll soon be marching into this town in search of your head.

WHITNEY. Why should they? He's a confessed spy—

SCHAEFER. He's one of our own, Mr. Whitney, he did it for reasons we all understand—

WHITNEY. Which is the real truth about you, isn't it?

SCHAEFER. I beg your pardon?

WHITNEY. You claim to be loyal Americans, but when it comes to a choice, your loyalty is to each other, not to the United States—

FITZGERALD. Whitney, do you know what you are saying?

WHITNEY. Yes I do. (*To Schaefer.*) And all your money and your pressure won't make a difference this time. You're dealing with the Department of Justice now, not some craven politicians—

DAVID. Whitney, I'm warning you—

WHITNEY. I have the full support of my superiors on this, it comes right from the top! We will not budge on David Klein, not one bloody inch!

FITZGERALD. Then you be sure and tell your "superiors" to watch TV tonight. I don't want them to miss the report that my subcommittee will be investigating charges that the Justice Department is being run by a bunch of anti-semitic racists!

WHITNEY. You won't do that—

FITZGERALD. Won't I? When I get through it won't be the Justice Department! It'll be an outplacement service for unemployed lawyers! Let's get out of here, Arthur ...

(*FITZGERALD and SCHAEFER exit. BLACKOUT. The sound of a TRAIN passing close by, almost a roar. A WHISTLE blows.*)

Scene 2

LIGHTS UP on EZRA sitting on the Metroliner. SCHAEFER enters and sits across from Ezra.

The sound of the TRAIN fades into the background.

EZRA. We should have taken the shuttle ...

SCHAEFER. We want to get there, don't we?

EZRA. I'm not sure.

SCHAEFER. I don't blame you. There's going to be some very angry Jews at this meeting ...

EZRA. I am upset myself.

SCHAEFER. I still don't understand what happened.

EZRA. I told you everything I know. The Cabinet decided yesterday to object to certain terms and conditions of the Justice Department.

SCHAEFER. It was all worked out and agreed to. How can they just change their minds?

EZRA. They did it evidently in their last discussions with us—

SCHAEFER. I'm talking about your Cabinet.

EZRA. (*Pause.*) The Justice Department is saying now they want to extradite him to the United States—

SCHAEFER. That's what they were always saying—

EZRA. It was for U.S. representatives to question him in Tel Aviv—

SCHAEFER. In order to determine if extradition was warranted. But we all knew that was just a formality.

EZRA. I think you are mistaken—

SCHAEFER. I'm the one who put this deal together. How can they just change their minds like that without telling me?

EZRA. It is a policy question, not personal—

SCHAEFER. It's personal to me.

EZRA. (*Pause.*) Arthur, no one can say you did not do enough for David Klein. But I will also tell the Jewish leadership tonight, this is a matter now of Israel's security, not a question for public debate—

SCHAEFER. You want me to shut up? Like you wanted Rachel Klein to shut up?

EZRA. American Jews have a moral duty to support the decisions of Israel in relations with a foreign government—

SCHAEFER. What foreign government?

EZRA. The United States—

SCHAEFER. That's not a foreign government to us.

EZRA. (*Pause.*) Arthur, I am upset by this as you, believe me.

SCHAEFER. So what happens now?

EZRA. There are people working in Israel, forces, for the same goal as ours. Yesterday those who wish not to be seen giving in to American pressure were the majority but—

SCHAEFER. What American pressure?

EZRA. The use of David Klein for blackmail against Israel.

SCHAEFER. You know that's not what's going on—

EZRA. All I am saying to you is what I was explained today from Jerusalem. The Cabinet is divided. It will take time to change enough positions ...

SCHAEFER. How much time?

EZRA. This I cannot know for sure.

SCHAEFER. David's already on his way to prison ...

EZRA. I know.

SCHAEFER. To Petersburg, which is not the easiest place ...

EZRA. This is not a decision I can affect.

SCHAEFER. We've got half the American Jewish leadership coming to his meeting tonight. What if we write a letter, or send a delegation?

EZRA. This would only make it more hard for the Cabinet to show weakness—

SCHAEFER. It's not a question of weakness, it's a question of fairness!

EZRA. I am only saying, as you say yourself all the time, such questions are better to answer in a quiet way.

SCHAEFER. Are you sure they'll change their position?

EZRA. It is the right thing to do.

SCHAEFER. And what am I supposed to tell the Kleins?

EZRA. To be patient, to see this is only a delay.

SCHAEFER. I'm sure they'll believe that ...

EZRA. (Pause.) Arthur, please do not say to anyone that we discussed this? If I as the ambassador was known to say such things about decisions of my government ...

SCHAEFER. I won't get you in trouble, you know that.

EZRA. And you will keep them calm tonight?

SCHAEFER. I'll try to keep them from tearing you to pieces, if that's what you mean ...

EZRA. You think they will be violent?

SCHAEFER. This is the Jewish leadership, Ezra. The only thing they know how to hurt are your feelings.

(*The TRAIN WHISTLE blows and SCHAEFER goes downstage. LIGHTS fade except for a single SPOT on Schaefer.*)

Scene 3

SCHAEFER. (*Speaks to the audience.*) It has been said, the comparison has been made, to the Rosenbergs.

(*EZRA exits.*)

SCHAEFER. That they did it, yes, but they didn't deserve to die for it. After all, we let murderers and rapists back on the streets every day. Drug dealers walk around with machine guns under their arms and we don't even arrest them. But David Klein we put in jail for the rest of his life. Now something like this, another Rosenberg case, you would think the Jews would be up in arms. How many times does it happen, some teenagers paint swastikas on a synagogue, and the great American Jewish outrage machine cranks up at a moment's notice. For a kid who gets sent to prison for the rest of his life because he wanted to be a Jewish hero, you would expect a noise like no one ever heard. But in the days and weeks after David was sentenced, there was not one word of protest from the Jewish community.

(*FITZGERALD enters and sits behind his desk.*)

SCHAEFER. Not ... one ... word ... (*Turns to Fitzgerald.*)

Scene 4

LIGHTS up on Fitzgerald's office in the Capitol. TELEPHONES and OFFICE MACHINES can be heard offstage.

SCHAEFER. Is that all he said, that he has a new offer?
FITZGERALD. Which will solve the problem. That's what he told me.
SCHAEFER. He better be right ...
FITZGERALD. How is David holding up?
SCHAEFER. I don't think very well ...

FITZGERALD. Let's hope we can get him out of Petersburg soon.

SCHAEFER. That would help ...

(*The PHONE rings on Fitzgerald's desk. HE answers it.*)

FITZGERALD. (*Into the phone.*) Yes? ... They are? Good. Send them in ... And don't forget to hold the calls until we're finished. (*HE hangs up.*)

SCHAEFER. Who's here?

FITZGERALD. Both of them.

SCHAEFER. I still think David's lawyers should be here too ...

FITZGERALD. Whitney insisted. Besides, you don't want lawyers around at a time like this. They always think they have something to contribute ...

(*EZRA and WHITNEY enter.*)

FITZGERALD. Gentlemen, come in.

WHITNEY. Congressman ...

FITZGERALD. You both know Rabbi Schaefer.

EZRA. Arthur.

WHITNEY. Congressman, I'm on a very tight schedule.

(*THEY all sit.*)

FITZGERALD. So let's get started right away. I don't have to tell anyone here this is a very serious problem. It may not be on page one every day, but relations between our countries are as tense as I've ever seen them.

EZRA. There are unfortunately many more enemies of Israel here than we had thought—

FITZGERALD. It's not a question of enemies, Ezra, it's a question of reaching an understanding among friends—

EZRA. Frank, with all respect, this problem continues for one reason. Because of people who would rather see distrust between the United States and Israel, in spite of the mutual benefits—

FITZGERALD. And we're all aware of those benefits, which is why we need to resolve this. Now you told me you have something new for us...?

EZRA. As we have said before, and many times, the State of Israel regrets this distraction of relations between our countries—

WHITNEY. "Distraction"? You mean, "disruption"?

FITZGERALD. Whitney ...

EZRA. This disruption of relations. We will therefore take the following steps. Not because we were involved in any way, but strictly as a gesture of humanity for an effort that was made on our behalf. Misguided, of course. (*Reading from a sheet of paper.*) "The government of Israel will pay all legal expenses for the defense of David Klein."

FITZGERALD. That's very generous.

EZRA. (*Reading:*) "Also, the Deputy Foreign Minister of Israel will answer all written questions about this matter from the United States Justice Department and provide written answers to the best of his knowledge."

FITZGERALD. Go on ...

EZRA. (*Folding the paper.*) These are Israel's concessions.

WHITNEY. (*Pause.*) That's what you call "concessions"?

FITZGERALD. Now, Win—

WHITNEY. You expect us to let a spy out of prison in exchange for some written answers—?

EZRA. You will have all answers to questions affecting United States security—

WHITNEY. We need the man who ran the operation.

EZRA. There was no operation. There was only the single incident of David Klein—

WHITNEY. (*To Fitzgerald.*) You see, Congressman, they still refuse to cooperate—

EZRA. We do cooperate!

WHITNEY. How can you say that with a straight face?

FITZGERALD. Win, please. Ezra. I think we should all calm down—

(*The PHONE rings. FITZGERALD picks it up.*)

FITZGERALD. (*Shouting into the phone.*) Didn't I say, no calls! (*HE slams the phone down*.) Excuse me. Now Win, I know you told your people about this meeting ...

WHITNEY. Yes I did, and the Attorney General instructed me to come here today with a new proposal of our own, to show that at least the Department of Justice is dealing in good faith ...

FITZGERALD. So let's hear it...

WHITNEY. We are now prepared to forego formal extradition, although Israel agreed to it previously—

EZRA. We never agreed to extradite—

FITZGERALD. Ezra, please. Let's hear the proposal.

WHITNEY. As I was saying if this man Ephra ... Ephra ...

EZRA. Ephraim

WHITNEY. (*Pause*.) If he will voluntarily appear before the grand jury—

EZRA. That is no change!

WHITNEY. The Department will recommend to the court that David Klein's prison term be substantially reduced.

SCHAEFER. How substantially?

WHITNEY. The original terms, fifteen years, ten suspended, parole after two ...

SCHAEFER. In a better prison?

WHITNEY. He'll be moved to Danbury on the day this man completes his testimony—

EZRA. (*On his feet*.) We cannot allow such blackmail!

SCHAEFER. It isn't blackmail—

EZRA. The State of Israel is anxious to help the United States government resolve its security problems—

WHITNEY. The State of Israel is the problem—!

EZRA. But we cannot discuss with people who are concerned only to put more Jews in jail—

WHITNEY. Our only concern is to learn the truth—

EZRA. We offer the truth—

WHITNEY. Directly from the man who recruited David Klein in the first place—

EZRA. There was no recruitment!

FITZGERALD. Gentlemen—

EZRA. David Klein acted on his own will!

WHITNEY. We just want you to prove that to us—

FITZGERALD. Gentlemen—!

EZRA. What you want is to do harm to Israel—

WHITNEY. (*Standing.*) How dare you make that kind of accusation?

FITZGERALD. (*On his feet.*) Gentlemen, gentlemen, please! (*Pause.*) Now I for one think there's room here to work out a compromise.

WHITNEY. Well I for one don't see it.

EZRA. Of course not.

FITZGERALD. Let's go over it point by point—

WHITNEY. Congressman, twice now, we've made a generous offer. Many would say, too

generous. And twice now our supposedly loyal
ally has shown no interest whatsoever—

EZRA. Who is not a loyal ally?

WHITNEY. That's perfectly clear.

EZRA. Who is not loyal is the so-called super-
power that relies on a small country to defend its
interests in a critical region of the world, but will
not share the weapons we need to defend
ourselves.

SCHAEFER. Ezra, that's not the issue—

EZRA. It is the issue! This is why David Klein
thought to give these plans to Israel, that his own
government would not, in spite of a written
agreement it will do so. Because of people in the
United States government who want Jewish blood
as always—

WHITNEY. Now that's bullshit!

FITZGERALD. Win!

(*EZRA goes to the door.*)

SCHAEFER. Ezra, where you going—?

EZRA. The State of Israel is fully willing to
make agreements for the sake of good relations
with an important ally. But we do not submit to
blackmail. Not from terrorists, and not from
Americans. Gentlemen.

SCHAEFER. Ezra—!

(*EZRA exits.*)

WHITNEY. Congressman, if I may point out, the Justice Department remains flexible and willing to compromise. I trust you'll take that into account regarding these hearings of yours. Gentlemen. (*Exits.*)

FITZGERALD. (*Long pause.*) Well. That was certainly productive.

SCHAEFER. Don't they realize there are lives at stake?

FITZGERALD. Lives are always at stake in politics. Most of the time we have the good fortune not to know the people personally ...

SCHAEFER. That's pretty cynical, Frank.

FITZGERALD. I'm not the one who's leaving David Klein to rot in jail.

SCHAEFER. That Whitney is pretty unpleasant—

FITZGERALD. I'm not talking about Whitney. I'm trying to understand why the Israelis are taking this position and the only answer I come up with is they want it buried. And they don't care if David gets buried too.

SCHAEFER. I can't believe that.

FITZGERALD. I know you can't. But I have to be honest with you, Arthur. A lot of people in this town are starting to ask, if the Jews don't care about David Klein, why should we?

SCHAEFER. Of course we care!

FITZGERALD. I told Whitney there'd be a million angry people in the streets, remember? Right after the sentencing? Where are they?

SCHAEFER. I know the outcry is a bit restrained ...

FITZGERALD. There is no outcry. None at all.

SCHAEFER. Nobody's sure what to do ...

FITZGERALD. Arthur! Arthur! Whenever any one of us in this town does something you don't like you know exactly what to do. You let us have it with both barrels ...

SCHAEFER. This is different—

FITZGERALD. Because it's them? Israeli politicians never make mistakes?

SCHAEFER. Of course they do—

FITZGERALD. But you can't come out and say so? What are you afraid of?

SCHAEFER. I'm not.

FITZGERALD. Not even the truth?

(*A BUZZER sounds.*)

FITZGERALD. That's a roll call. I have to get to the floor for a vote ...

SCHAEFER. What do we do next, Frank?

FITZGERALD. That, my friend, is up to you—

SCHAEFER. I'll talk to Ezra—

FITZGERALD. Ezra is just a mouthpiece.

SCHAEFER. I'll go to Israel then ...

FITZGERALD. For what? Arthur, you're supposed to be a leader.

SCHAEFER. (*Pause.*) What are you suggesting?

FITZGERALD. The Justice Department wants someone to admit that Israel recruited David Klein—

SCHAEFER. They didn't.

FITZGERALD. You still think David took those plans all by himself?

SCHAEFER. (*Pause.*) I'm not sure what I think ...

FITZGERALD. Well maybe you should ask him. Because he knows. And he better tell you real soon, before it's too late. (*Exits.*)

(*SCHAEFER goes downstage. LIGHTS to black except for a single SPOT on Schaefer*)

Scene 5

SCHAEFER. (*Speaks to the audience.*) Suddenly I found myself thinking of Abraham, the father of the Jews. How when God tells him, "Take your son Isaac to the mountains and make a sacrifice," he packs up and gets going right away, no questions asked. And not just because a Jew will jump at any chance to go to the mountains.

(*RACHEL enters and waits in the visiting room of the prison.*)

SCHAEFER. On the way, Abraham wonders, "What exactly are we going to sacrifice?" And God says, "Don't worry." When Isaac asks the same question, Abraham tells him, "Don't worry." When they get to the top of the mountain, God says, "It's Isaac I want you to sacrifice." and what does Abraham do? He ties up Isaac on the altar, he picks up the knife, he's going to do it. God has to say, "No, no, wait, just kidding, just testing you." (*Pause.*) Just testing you. What amazes me is it never occurs to Abraham to ask, "What kind of a crazy test is that?" Which is maybe why God gave the Law to Moses. Let's face it, to be the father of the Jews, all Abraham needed was his reproductive system. Moses, with his arguing, with all his questions, is the one who got the Law.

(*LIGHTS down on SCHAEFER, who turns toward Rachel.*)

Scene 6

LIGHTS up on the visiting room of the prison. RACHEL is waiting at a table with a glass divider down the middle. On either side is a chair, and a telephone. DOORS clang in the background. There is shouting. A GUARD enters, followed by DAVID. SCHAEFER exits. DAVID is wearing prison clothes and

*handcuffs. HE walks slowly over to the table
and sits. The GUARD stands just inside the
door. RACHEL picks up the phone on her side
and waits until DAVID lifts his. THEY talk into
the phones.*

DAVID. You look wonderful ...
RACHEL. So do you ...
DAVID. I know how I look.
RACHEL. I mean, it's so good to see you. I
miss you so much.
DAVID. I miss you too ...
RACHEL. I can't wait to hold you again ...
Just to touch you ...
DAVID. Please.
RACHEL. I'm sorry ... I know it's harder for
you ... But you won't be in there for long ...
DAVID. Don't lie to me, Rachel ...
RACHEL. Rabbi Schaefer says it'll just take a
little time—
DAVID. Is that what he says ...?
RACHEL. There's a lot of pressure building
up in Israel, people demonstrating against the
government, demanding they do something to
help you .... There's a lot of outrage over there ...
DAVID. This prison's over here ...
RACHEL. We just have to give it some time.
DAVID. I have plenty of that, don't I? A
lifetime ...
RACHEL. David ...
DAVID. My mother was here. She hasn't
heard from you since the sentencing.

RACHEL. You know how she is ...

DAVID. I asked you to stay in touch with her. She's all alone—

RACHEL. So am I—

DAVID. But she's lost so much. First my father, now me ...

RACHEL. David, you're just in here, and just for now.

(*Pause.*)

DAVID. (*Glancing at the guard.*) It's really bad in here ... You read about prison, you get this picture of being alone in a cell, all this silence, nobody to talk to ... That's how I always imagined it ... But it's so loud ... Even at night, you never get a chance to think, so much clanging, and banging ... When I think of spending the rest of my life in here—

RACHEL. You won't have to—

DAVID. Rachel, there's something I want you to do for me.

RACHEL. Anything, you know that—

DAVID. I've asked the lawyers to prepare some papers.

RACHEL. What papers?

DAVID. For a divorce.

RACHEL. (*Pause.*) What are you talking about?

DAVID. I want a divorce—

RACHEL. Because I didn't see your mother?

DAVID. I'm not joking—

RACHEL. I'll call her this afternoon, okay?

DAVID. I don't love you anymore—

RACHEL. Of course you do—

DAVID. So there's no reason you should ruin the rest of your life—

RACHEL. David, you are my life—

DAVID. You just have to sign the papers—

RACHEL. You're being ridiculous!

DAVID. And send them back, the lawyers will do the rest—

RACHEL. I won't—

DAVID. The divorce will go through in a few weeks and—

RACHEL. (*Pounds her phone on the table.*) Can't you hear through this?

DAVID. Why are you so stubborn?

RACHEL. Why are you?

DAVID. That I don't want you wasting your life—

RACHEL. I already did, I married you! (*SHE smiles.*) I love you, David, you know that. And you love me, too. Remember? (*Pause.*) Do you remember?

DAVID. Yes.

RACHEL. Don't ever forget ...

(*RACHEL puts her hand on the glass. DAVID places his hand against hers.*)

DAVID. That's the worst thing about it, what I did to you ...

RACHEL. You didn't do anything to me—

DAVID. You should be having children—

RACHEL. We will—

DAVID. Not a husband in jail the rest of his life—

RACHEL. You won't be. They had a meeting, David, at the beginning of the week—

DAVID. Who did?

RACHEL. All of them. Schaefer, Whitney, Fitzgerald, Ben-Ami—

DAVID. You can't expect me to make another deal, after what happened ...

RACHEL. It's the only way you'll get out—

DAVID. (*On his feet.*) Then I won't get out!

(*The guard turns toward him.*)

RACHEL. (*Quietly, watching the guard.*) David, sit down ...

(*DAVID sits. The guard turns away.*)

DAVID. Next week is Hanukkah ...

RACHEL. I know.

DAVID. That was always my father's favorite Jewish holiday ... He called it the holiday of heroes ...

RACHEL. (*With him.*) ... "the holiday of heroes" ...

DAVID. But he never let me get presents like the other kids. He always gave me everything I wanted, all I had to do was ask. But not on Hanukkah ...

RACHEL. I remember ...

DAVID. He didn't want to detract from what we were celebrating, how the Maccabees were willing to sacrifice their lives for Israel ... (*Pause.*) That's how I was brought up, Rachel, I won't be able to live with myself if I—

RACHEL. Well it isn't up to you. There's nothing you can do to stop them, whatever they decide to do they'll do ...

DAVID. Over my dead body.

RACHEL. (*Pause.*) That isn't funny, David ...

DAVID. I'm not being funny.

RACHEL. (*Pause.*) What are you saying?

DAVID. It's the solution to everybody's problems ...

RACHEL. Don't talk like that—

DAVID. I want you to tell them, Rachel—

RACHEL. Stop it! You sound like a child! When are you going to realize they don't give a damn what you want, or what you do, or what happens to you. I'm the only one who cares about you! (*Pause.*) The only one ... (*Pause.*)

GUARD. Time.

DAVID. I have to go. (*HE stands.*)

RACHEL. David—

DAVID. I have to go. (*Puts down his phone and walks toward the door.*)

RACHEL. (*Shouting.*) All right! All right! (*Pause.*) I'll tell them ... I'll tell them ...

(*DAVID returns to the table and picks up his phone.*)

RACHEL. I'll tell them not to make another deal ... All right?

DAVID. (*Pause.*) And you'll talk to my mother...?

RACHEL. I'll call her ...

DAVID. See her?

RACHEL. (*Pause. With forced cheerfulness.*) You see how much I love you?

DAVID. Yes ...

RACHEL. I'll tell her how good you look.

DAVID. Don't lie ...

RACHEL. No. I won't lie.

GUARD. Let's go.

RACHEL. I'll be back next week ...

DAVID. Goodbye, Rachel. (*Puts down his phone, kisses his fingers and touches the glass. HE stops at the door, looks back at Rachel, then exits, followed by the guard.*)

RACHEL. I love you ... (*Drops her phone and covers her face in her hands. The LIGHTS fade to black.*)

Scene 7

LIGHTS up on the patio behind the Kleins' home. There is a tea service on a small table next to a chair. Offstage, winter BIRDS can be heard. HELEN enters, wrapping a shawl around her. After a moment, SHE sits. SCHAEFER enters.

SCHAEFER. It's freezing out here.

HELEN. I wasn't expecting anyone.

SCHAEFER. The maid let me in. Helen, I have to talk to you—

HELEN. What is there to talk about?

SCHAEFER. David. I think Israel recruited him—

HELEN. I know they did. (*Pause*.) David told me.

SCHAEFER. You didn't tell me—

HELEN. Why should I?

SCHAEFER. I'm trying to help you—

HELEN. There's nothing you can do to help.

SCHAEFER. (*Pause*.) They lied to me, Helen...

HELEN. Of course they lied to you.

SCHAEFER. I didn't want to believe it, but it's true ...

HELEN. Is that why you came here? To tell me that?

SCHAEFER. We have to talk to David. He has to admit that Israel recruited him. Then Israel will have to produce Ephraim, and the judge will reduce his sentence ...

HELEN. You make it sound so simple.

SCHAEFER. It is simple. We just have to convince him—

HELEN. What makes you think he'll listen?

SCHAEFER. He will, to you—

HELEN. He won't.

SCHAEFER. I've never seen a mother and son as close as you and David.

HELEN. We were. Before he lied to me.

SCHAEFER. He had to, it's part of that world—

HELEN. He never should have been in that world! It was Sam, constantly filling his head with stories of Jewish heroes ...

SCHAEFER. You can't blame this on Sam—

HELEN. I warned David not to make the same mistake, not to let other people use him for their own ends, as Sam did—

SCHAEFER. Nobody used Sam.

HELEN. The two of you. Like children, playing heroes. Thinking you were world-class operators. You were pawns. They let you feel important as long as you did what they wanted. As soon as they don't need you anymore, it's as if you never existed.

SCHAEFER. That doesn't matter now. All that matters is getting David out of prison ...

HELEN. Please. I'd like you to leave me alone.

SCHAEFER. Why can't I get through to you? I speak to you, I listen, but I never know what you're thinking. It's as if there's a wall around you, around your feelings ...

HELEN. I am not that complicated. I am a widow. My only child is in prison. Everything important to me is gone.

SCHAEFER. David isn't gone—

HELEN. It's as if Sam reached right out of his grave and took him away from me—

SCHAEFER. Goddammit, Helen!

SCHAEFER. (*Knocks over the tea service and it crashes to the ground.*) You have no right to feel so sorry for yourself!

HELEN. Go away from me ...

SCHAEFER. And you have no right to let David sit in prison just because he didn't do what you wanted him to do.

HELEN. How dare you—!

SCHAEFER. He was just trying to be like his father, who was a hero whether you admit it or not. It's just that nobody wants heroes anymore. But that isn't David's fault. We have to make him understand he's wrong to sacrifice his life for politics—

HELEN. You're the one who never understood. You're the one who always put politics ahead of everyone.

SCHAEFER. I was wrong.

HELEN. It's a little late for you to find that out, now that my life is ruined. And David's.

SCHAEFER. We can still save David's life! And that's what's important!

(*Pause, then RACHEL enters from the house. She is wearing a dark dress, and her hair is pulled back severely.*)

SCHAEFER. Rachel ...

RACHEL. (*Looking at the remains of the tea service.*) What happened?

HELEN. Nothing. An accident. I wasn't expecting you.

RACHEL. David asked me to come—

HELEN. He did?

RACHEL. He thought you might like a visitor. I didn't realize you had one ...

SCHAEFER. How is David?

RACHEL. Spending his life in prison, how should he be?

SCHAEFER. (*Going to her.*) Rachel, we have to talk to him—

RACHEL. (*Avoiding him.*) There's nothing to say—

SCHAEFER. He has to admit he was recruited—

RACHEL. Who told you that?

SCHAEFER. I'm no genius but even I can figure out I'm being lied to—

RACHEL. It doesn't matter.

SCHAEFER. It does. The Justice Department is under a lot of pressure, David just has to tell them the truth—

RACHEL. He won't.

SCHAEFER. We have to convince him—

RACHEL. You can't—

SCHAEFER. The three of us—

RACHEL. No!

SCHAEFER. (*Pause.*) Rachel, what's wrong with you?

RACHEL. David and I would prefer if you did nothing more to help us.

SCHAEFER. You were the one who asked me in the first place—

RACHEL. Yes, well now I want you to stop.

SCHAEFER. (*Pause.*) You want David to spend the rest of his life in prison?

RACHEL. At least he'll be alive. (*Pause.*) If you make another deal, David will kill himself.

HELEN. He said that?

SCHAEFER. He's not that kind of man—

RACHEL. He is. Now he is. And he wants to you to stop.

SCHAEFER. What do you want?

RACHEL. I want him alive.

SCHAEFER. Rachel, you were the last one I expected to give up hope—

RACHEL. I'm sorry to disappoint you.

SCHAEFER. (*To Helen.*) Helen, help me convince her ...

HELEN. No. I also want him alive.

SCHAEFER. In prison? What kind of life is that?

RACHEL. The only kind of life he has left.

SCHAEFER. It's not. We can still get him out—

RACHEL. You can't.

SCHAEFER. Not if we give up hope! Well I won't give up—

RACHEL. Please! You have to stop—

SCHAEFER. I'm sorry, but I can't! (*Exits.*)

RACHEL. (*Pause.*) He has to stop ...

HELEN. It doesn't matter what he does. Nobody cares about David anymore ...
RACHEL. Except us ...
HELEN. Yes. Except for us.

(*RACHEL picks up the broken tea service and puts the pieces on the tray.*)

HELEN. You don't have to do that ...
RACHEL. I want to.

(*Pause.*)

(*Finished, RACHEL stands and starts to exit. HELEN stops her.*)

HELEN. Thank you.

(*RACHEL takes HELEN's hand a moment, then exits. Pause. HELEN exits. LIGHTS fade except for a single spot on SCHAEFER who enters downstage.*)

SCHAEFER. (*Speaks to the audience.*) I spoke before of Moses. You recall, he never did get to the Promised Land. That was the price he paid for all his complaining, all his questions. He had to turn things over to Joshua before they crossed the Jordan River. Now Joshua, we think of as a warrior, the man who conquered Canaan, who fought the battle of Jericho. But in the Bible, it was God, not Joshua, who actually brought down

the walls. All Joshua did was have his people
follow the priests around the city every day for six
days, carrying the ark of the covenant, shouting
and yelling and blowing their horns. Think of the
sight that must have been. These crazy Jews from
the desert parading around with their sheep and
their goats and their portable temple. No wonder
the Canaanites laughed, up on the walls of their
fancy city. Until the seventh day, when the
strange new God knocked the walls down flat.
(*Pause*.) Now Joshua today, with his charisma,
would have no trouble finding Jews to march
around, shouting and blowing their horns and
acting like heroes and getting on the six o'clock
news every night. But the walls would not come
down. Because who believes in God these days?
We Jews believe in politics and diplomacy, in
nations and leaders. We march around in circles
all our lives. And the walls stay right where they
are ... (*Walks upstage and waits*.)

Scene 9

*LIGHTS up on the gate of the Israeli Embassy.
Offstage, the sound of TRAFFIC. EZRA
comes out in a hurry, sees Schaefer and stops.*

EZRA. Arthur—?
SCHAEFER. I've been trying to see you since
yesterday.

EZRA. I cannot tell you how busy it is ...

SCHAEFER. I'm sure.

EZRA. Just now I am late for a reception at the Embassy of Brazil, I am waiting for my car—

SCHAEFER. We have to talk ...

EZRA. It would be better when there is more time—

SCHAEFER. It has to be now. (*Pause.*)

EZRA. Arthur, you don't look well.

SCHAEFER. I don't feel very well ...

EZRA. This has been difficult for all of us—

SCHAEFER. We have to get him out of prison...

EZRA. We have done everything we can—

SCHAEFER. His wife thinks he's suicidal ...

EZRA. I do not think so ...

SCHAEFER. We have to talk to him.

EZRA. "We"?

SCHAEFER. To convince him to tell the truth to the Justice Department—

EZRA. What truth?

SCHAEFER. That he was recruited.

EZRA. This is not so—

DAVID. Don't lie to me, Ezra—

EZRA. I do not lie.

SCHAEFER. You told me Ephraim was a private citizen. You told me David came in out of the blue with the plans. You told me you were cooperating with the Justice Department. Was any of that true?

EZRA. It is what I was told from Jerusalem—

SCHAEFER. So tell David they lied to you, too. Make him see he's not betraying Israel by telling the truth.

EZRA. Why would he listen to me?

SCHAEFER. You're the ambassador.

EZRA. If I tell him what you ask, I would betray Israel myself.

SCHAEFER. Ezra, they lied to you ...

EZRA. It is many times the obligation of an ambassador for his government to lie to him ...

SCHAEFER. What about your obligation to David?

EZRA. It is your Justice Department. They could let him out tomorrow, but all they want is that we will trade one Jew for another. This is something Israel can never do—

SCHAEFER. You trade with the Arabs after every war, you give up hundreds of prisoners just to get your corpses back ...

EZRA. It is a question of security—

SCHAEFER. No, Ezra, no. It's a question of responsibility. Your government has to admit its mistakes.

EZRA. Arthur, this is what the gentiles wanted all along. To divide us—

SCHAEFER. You divided us. You took advantage of David's loyalty and now you're letting him take the blame—

EZRA. You sound like Wingate Whitney—

SCHAEFER. You told me they would do what was right. Remember, on the Metroliner?

EZRA. They believe they are—

SCHAEFER. Do you believe they are?

EZRA. The United States government continues to recognize the importance of Israel in its geopolitical strategy—

SCHAEFER. I'm not talking about geopolitics—

EZRA. Better you should not.

SCHAEFER. I'm talking one Jew to another, one human being to another. Sam Klein was our friend. This is his son. We can't let him die in there ...

EZRA. He is very tough, David Klein—

SCHAEFER. He's not—

EZRA. I did not think Americans could be so tough.

SCHAEFER. I didn't think Israelis could be so cruel.

EZRA. The State of Israel does what is best for the Jewish people—

SCHAEFER. Isn't David one of the Jewish people?

EZRA. There are always casualties in war—

SCHAEFER. It's not his war.

EZRA. He is a Jew—

SCHAEFER. He's an American.

EZRA. Arthur? Always before, it was your war, too.

SCHAEFER. And no one is more committed to Jewish survival than I am. You know how much I've done—

EZRA. What?

SCHAEFER. How much I've sacrificed—

EZRA. What have you sacrificed? You did not come to live in Israel, you stay comfortable in America, while we build the country and fight the wars and make you proud and impress the gentiles for you! Until the day comes when the gentiles are not so impressed, and suddenly, it is not your war anymore ...

SCHAEFER. How can you say this to me?

EZRA. You should take the example of David Klein yourself. He put his life in danger, and stays now in prison without complaining. This is what it is to sacrifice—

SCHAEFER. When people find out about this—

EZRA. What people?

SCHAEFER. Americans, Ezra. Jews—

EZRA. They do not care.

SCHAEFER. Don't kid yourself—

EZRA. Look in your newspapers, Arthur, on your television. Where is David Klein? Forgotten. In Israel, he is a hero. But here, you want to forget, because it reminds you, for all your money and your great success, America is not so different. You live in fear of gentiles here, just as Jews in Russia, or Iran ...

SCHAEFER. Don't be ridiculous—

EZRA. Look at your own reaction, when the news came out. Your first reaction was, "What will the goyim think?"

SCHAEFER. And you have the most powerful lobby in Washington because you don't care what they think?

EZRA. As an independent nation—
SCHAEFER. "Independent"? The day the dollars stop rolling in, your "independent nation" is out of business!
EZRA. As always with Americans it becomes a question of money—
SCHAEFER. It's not a question of money! And it's not a question of fear! It's a question of a boy's life being sacrificed for politics ...

(*The sound of a CAR pulling up.*)

EZRA. Here is my car ... (*HE starts off.*)
SCHAEFER. Ezra!
EZRA. (*Pause. Turning back to Schaefer.*) I am sorry, Arthur. Truly. I wish the best for David Klein.
SCHAEFER. Ezra, please—

(*EZRA exits. LIGHTS fade. SCHAEFER doesn't move.*)

Scene 10

LIGHTS up on a small room off the chapel of the prison. The sound of distant CLANGING DOORS and, closer but still in the background, MEN reciting prayers in Latin. DAVID enters behind SCHAEFER, wearing handcuffs, looking dulled and almost dead.

DAVID. You—?

SCHAEFER. (*Turning to him.*) How are you, David?

DAVID. They didn't tell me it was you—

SCHAEFER. They must've wanted it to be a surprise ... I brought you something.

DAVID. What?

(*SCHAEFER takes a book out of his pocket and offers it to DAVID, who doesn't take it.*)

DAVID. It's a Bible.

DAVID. What's that for?

SCHAEFER. What else should a rabbi bring?

DAVID. Since when are you a rabbi?

SCHAEFER. I'm trying to be.

DAVID. No more big-shot wheeler-dealer?

SCHAEFER. Look inside, the inscription. (*Puts the book in David's hands.*)

DAVID. (*Opens it.*) Sharansky.

SCHAEFER. He wrote that when I met him. I want you to have it.

DAVID. It's to you ...

SCHAEFER. I know he's one of your heroes. Did you read what he wrote in his book about "the interconnectedness of souls"?

DAVID. I read it.

SCHAEFER. Where he says that's how he survived in prison, that spiritual connection to his wife and his family and his people, how it gave him something to live for—

DAVID. I read it.

SCHAEFER. I realize now that's the meaning of Jewish history, of our survival. The interconnectedness of souls. That's why it hurts me so much to see what they're doing to you.

DAVID. Don't make me out to be some kind of victim. I made my own decisions, I'm nobody's victim—

SCHAEFER. You're not the only one responsible, either.

DAVID. (*Starts to prowl the room nervously.*) Where are the dividers?

SCHAEFER. What?

DAVID. Everyone else I see has to be in this room with glass dividers.

SCHAEFER. The privileges of clergy, I suppose. Rachel told me you're having a difficult time here ...

DAVID. It's not so bad.

SCHAEFER. I still think we can get your sentence reduced—

DAVID. Did Rachel tell you no more deals—?

SCHAEFER. We haven't made another deal.

DAVID. (*Pause.*) Good.

SCHAEFER. Israel agrees with you. They prefer that you spend the rest of your life in prison. That way Ephraim doesn't have to tell the truth ...

DAVID. (*Pause. Turning away.*) They have to do what's best for the Jewish people. They can't worry about me.

SCHAEFER. There's an old saying, David. "Save one life, you save the whole world ..."

DAVID. I've heard it.

SCHAEFER. It's the same thing Sharansky is talking about. That people are more important than politics.

DAVID. You're the one who always said that Israel was more important than anything ...

SCHAEFER. I know that. I was wrong.

DAVID. You weren't wrong. (*Pause.*) Do you know that you were a hero to me, when I was growing up? You and my father, rushing around the world defending the Jewish people ... I wanted to be just like you ... And now you want me to betray Israel—

SCHAEFER. I want you to save your life—

DAVID. You don't know anything about my life—

SCHAEFER. How can you say that? I married your parents, I married you and Rachel, I conducted your bris, and your bar mitzvah. And your father's funeral. David, we're the interconnected souls that Sharansky is talking about, you and me and your father and mother and Rachel. It's not just your life involved in this, it's all the lives you're connected to. That's what Sharansky is talking about, that's why he let them make a deal to get him out.

DAVID. He wasn't asked to betray his people!

SCHAEFER. His people never betrayed him.

DAVID. (*Pause.*) I never thought I'd hear you talk like this.

SCHAEFER. I never thought I would either. (*Pause.*) David, you have to tell them that Israel recruited you—

DAVID. They didn't.

SCHAEFER. I know they did. And I'm not the only one, the prosecutors know it too. They just want someone to admit it. Israel won't. If you do, they'll reduce your sentence like they promised—

DAVID. Is that why you came here? Just to tell me that again?

SCHAEFER. It's the only hope we have left. Everyone else has abandoned you.

DAVID. Why won't you abandon me? Why is this so goddamn important to you?

SCHAEFER. Your father was important to me.

DAVID. My father has been dead for five years! Why didn't you owe him anything till now?

SCHAEFER. I didn't think your mother wanted to see me—

DAVID. What about me? Did you ever think maybe I wanted to see you?

SCHAEFER. (*Pause.*) I didn't ...

DAVID. And now you want me to turn on Israel just to make you feel better?

SCHAEFER. That's not the reason. David, I know you wanted to be a hero. Like your father, like Sharansky. But they aren't the same kinds of hero. In your father's day, a Jewish hero risked his life to defend the state. Today a hero has to defend life against the state. Just like Sharansky did.

DAVID. Why don't you take your speeches and your Bibles and your deals and leave me alone. (*Throws the Bible at Schaefer. It falls to the floor and HE stares at it.*)

SCHAEFER. (*Picks up the Bible and kisses it.*) I will. As soon as this is over I'll just disappear.

DAVID. It is over.

SCHAEFER. (*Pause.*) David, you're not that foolish—

DAVID. I'm tired of making everyone unhappy...

SCHAEFER. You think they won't be unhappy?

DAVID. They'll get over it—

SCHAEFER. They won't—

DAVID. Eventually—

SCHAEFER. Has your mother gotten over your father?

DAVID. We all know I'm not my father.

SCHAEFER. And Rachel? They way she loves you? She doesn't deserve it—

DAVID. She doesn't deserve to be living out there like a widow who can't go through shiva—

SCHAEFER. Of course she can't—

DAVID. Isn't the purpose of shiva for the living to get over the dead?

SCHAEFER. You're still alive—

DAVID. She needs to go through shiva—

SCHAEFER. She needs you to love her as much as she loves you! Do you love her that much?

DAVID. (*Goes to the door and bangs on it.*) Finished in here!

DAVID. David, listen to me—

DAVID. Finished in here!

SCHAEFER. If you won't tell the truth about this, I will!

DAVID. (*Pause.*) What are you talking about?

SCHAEFER. I'll tell your story in public—

DAVID. Why would anyone believe you?

SCHAEFER. You think people won't believe a rabbi attacking Israel?

DAVID. You won't do that—

SCHAEFER. I will. So you might as well tell them yourself—

DAVID. I swear to God, you say one word in public and—

SCHAEFER. What? You'll kill yourself? Go right ahead. And the very next day, I'll call a press conference and tell your story to the world.

DAVID. (*Pause.*) Why are you doing this to me?

SCHAEFER. I'm doing it for you...

DAVID. No ... (*HE bangs on the door again.*) Finished in here!

SCHAEFER. David, please—

DAVID. Finished—!

SCHAEFER. David—!

(*DAVID exits. SCHAEFER doesn't move for a long moment. Then HE goes to the podium. LIGHTS fade except for a single spot on Schaefer.*)

Scene 11

SCHAEFER. (*Speaks to the audience.*) The
rabbis tell us the questions are more imporant than
the answers. Ever since the Second World War,
we all believed we had the answers, we all *knew*,
after Auschwitz, that Israel was the answer to the
horrors of our history. Whatever the question,
Israel's survival was the answer. And as long as
that was your answer, then you were a Jew.

(*LIGHTS up on DAVID, sitting upstage, holding
    something.*)

SCHAEFER. Is it any wonder David Klein
believed us? That he acted on it? We said so many
times, we believed it so completely, we were so
sure of our answers, it never occurred to us that
maybe the questions could change. That maybe,
in a world of nuclear bombs and brushfire wars
and terrorist attacks, maybe nine million Jews in
Israel and America have as good a chance of
survival as any other people. Which means that
survival itself may not be enough of an answer
anymore. We may also have to ask ourselves,
survival for what?

DAVID. (*Stands. The LIGHTS fade on
Schaefer. DAVID steps up onto the chair.*) Shema
israel adonai elohenu adonai echod. (*HE is*

holding a noose, which *HE* throws over a pipe
above his head. *HE* pulls it tight, and puts his
head into it.)

(BLACKOUT)

End of Play

COSTUME PLOT

DAVID wears baggy pants, rumpled shirts in Act I, Scenes 1, 5 and 9, adding a jacket and tie in Scene 11. In Act II he wears prison clothes. Throughout he wears round, metal-framed glasses.

RACHEL wears jeans and a sweat shirt in Act I, Scenes 1, 5, and 9; a skirt and blouse in Scene 11 and in Act II, Scene 6; with an overcoat in Act II, Scene 7.

SCHAEFER wears a navy blue three-piece suit and a dark tie throughout, carrying an overcoat where appropriate, which he puts on for Act II, Scenes 7, 8, 9.

EZRA wears a poorly-fitted, inexpensive blue suit and dark tie, carrying or wearing a raincoat where appropriate.

HELEN wears finely-tailored, expensive dresses and suits, with a shawl in Act II, Scene 7.

FITZGERALD wears a blue suit, red bow tie and red suspenders. He can remove the jacket in Act II, Scene 4.

WHITNEY wears an expensive, conservative blue suit and a red or yellow tie.

The EMBASSY EMPLOYEE/ HEADWAITER /GUARD should dress appropriately for each role.

PROPERTY LIST

ACT I

Scene	Prop
2	EZRA enters with briefcase, umbrella
5	Plaque hung on wall; flowers on table; HELEN enters with eyeglasses and case; Two Philadelphia newspapers; Coffee service on a tray: coffee pot, sugar bowl, creamer, two cups and saucers, two spoons, napkin
7	On desk: blotter, desk calendar, pencil holder with pens and pencils, three books, papers, files, telephone, photos of wife and children WHITNEY enters with memo paper, pen
8	Cafeteria tray with two forks, two spoons, two plates with brown rice, glass of water, small juice container, two napkins
9	Tea service on tray: tea pot, sugar bowl, creamer, two cups and saucers, two spoons, napkin On table: magazines, Sharansky book (*Fear No Evil*), flowers. Plaque hung on wall. HELEN enters with eyeglasses and case

ACT II

Scene	Prop
1	On restaurant table: plate, fork, knife, spoon, salt and pepper shakers, ashtray, glass of wine (grape juice), napkin, menu, vase with flower
2	SCHAEFER enters with *Washington Post*
4	On desk: folders, papers, pens, telephone, small American flag in stand. EZRA enters with briefcase, pen, paper, pipe. WHITNEY enters with briefcase
6	On table: plexiglass divider with telephones on either side. DAVID enters wearing handcuffs
7	Tea service on tray: tea pot, sugar bowl, creamer, one cup and saucer, spoon, napkin
10	SCHAEFER enters with Bible. DAVID enters wearing handcuffs
11	DAVID enters with sheets tied in noose

Personal Props:

EZRA - umbrella, briefcase
HELEN - eyeglasses and case
WHITNEY - memo paper, pen

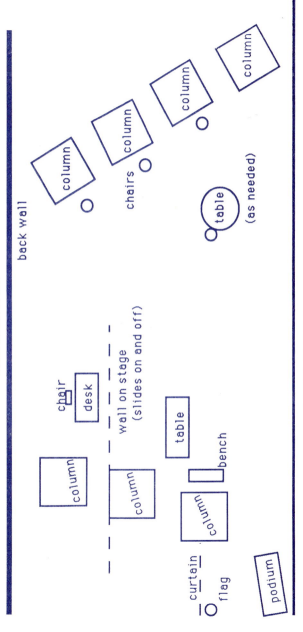

<<crossover>>

back wall

column

column

column

column

chairs

table (as needed)

wall on stage
(slides on and off)

chair

desk

table

bench

column

column

column

curtain

flag

podium

BITTER FRIENDS ground plan

THE
SAMUEL
FRENCH
THEATER
BOOKSHOP

Specializing in plays and
books on the theater

SAMUEL FRENCH, INC. (New York)
45 West 25th Street
New York, NY 10010
(212) 206-8990 (FAX 212-206-1429)
(open 9:00-5:00, Mon.-Fri.)

SAMUEL FRENCH, INC. (California)
7623 Sunset Blvd.   11963 Ventura Blvd.
Hollywood, CA 90045   Studio City, CA 91604
(213) 876-0570   (818) 762-0535
FAX 213-876-6822
        (call for hours)

SAMUEL FRENCH (Canada) LTD.
80 Richmond Street East
Toronto M5C 1P1
CANADA
(416) 363-3536
(open 9:00-5:00, Mon.-Fri.)

SAMUEL FRENCH LTD. (England)
52 Fitzroy Street
London W1P 6JR
England
011-441-387-9373   FAX 011-441-387-2161
(open 9:30-5:30, Mon.-Fri.)

ISBN 0 573 69201 7   #4176